# WATER

## THE ELIXIR OF LIFE

*Drink your way to greater health and happiness*

SANCTUARY PRESS

First published in Great Britain in 2014 by Sanctuary Press
an imprint of The Sanctuary of Healing

ISBN: 978-0-9928721-0-6

Typeset and designed by *in*zene, UK.
Printed and bound by Pioneer Print Solutions, UK.

The Sanctuary of Healing,
Dewhurst Road,
Langho, Blackburn,
Lancashire, BB6 8AF
United Kingdom

www.thesanctuaryofhealing.co.uk

# CONTENTS

Foreword                                    5
1: Introduction                             7
2: The Elixir of Life                      11
3: The Importance of Water                 15
4: Dehydration                             17
5: Gaining the Elixir                      25
6: Drought Management                      27
7: Emotions                                31
8: Natural Thirst                          33
9: Let's Take Action                       37
10: Water in all its Variety               41
11: Moving Inside                          49
12: The Hug in a Mug                       51
13: Good Vibrations                        53
14: Rounding Up                            57
About the Author                           60

'To my late father and to my mother.
Through thick and thin you have always been amazing in every way.
Thank you.'

## FOREWORD

The information within this book comes from knowledge I have learned over the years. My own ideas and beliefs have, in part, evolved from this knowledge, alongside my intuition and experiences. This book is written with very little reference to scientific research or statistics. Some empirical evidence is alluded to along the way. There are of course, many differing views about the majority of what I have written. We are all entitled to our own thoughts, feelings, beliefs and instincts about *Water*.

These are mine...

# 1

I don't know about you, but to me these two words 'self help' sound very dated, dull and almost patronising. However, we, as individuals, are without question, the best people to help ourselves. So many of us have been brought up to think that our health and happiness is actually not our responsibility. We rush to doctors and consultants in the hope that they will be able to 'fix' us and many of us believe that our health and happiness is to do with luck and therefore not really within our control, which is a very helpless state to be in. When, however, we start to realise and understand that it actually has nothing whatsoever to do with luck, then we become empowered because it means we can do something about it.

There are many wonderful disciplines, practices and therapies available to us. Amongst hundreds of others, I have enjoyed and benefited from quite a few of them – I'm talking about complementary/alternative therapies such as acupuncture, reflexology, reiki, homeopathy, EFT (emotional freedom technique), NLP (neuro linguistic programming), psych-K, massage/bodywork, all of which can be amazingly transformational given a good teacher or therapist or by learning the art ourselves. However, this book is not about going to other people to help us. It is about starting to take our power into our own hands and starting to take responsibility

## A VERY, VERY, WARM WELCOME TO YOU

I'm really delighted to meet you, figuratively speaking, and even more delighted that you have opened this book. I would love you to continue reading to the very end because I have so much to say and I can't say it all at once! I have enjoyed writing every word and have become even more fascinated, enthralled and spellbound by *Water* than ever before! I have delighted in incredible feelings of excitement bubbling up inside of me as I have made some life-changing realisations as this book has come together. I wish the same for you.

My aim has been to write this as I would speak it to you, so I invite you to make yourself comfy wherever you may be and we can have a good old natter...

for ourselves, our own health and wellbeing. It is also about learning about some things that we as individuals can do for ourselves, our physical, emotional and spiritual health without necessarily involving or relying on another person's help, skills, motivation or good nature.

Sadly, there are many people who live on Earth who do not have access to clean drinking *Water*. This is so incredibly devastating to their lives. Possibly after reading this book, some of you may feel encouraged to support the relevant charities/organisations who work to help to provide clean *Water* to areas of the world where it is often extremely polluted. For the much more fortunate of us, (and perhaps this is a good opportunity to truly appreciate our current *Water* supply no matter how far from perfect it is!) I hope that the practical things which I shall be talking about in this book will be affordable.

I'd like you to ask yourself, 'Am I feeling as energetic, flexible, alive and happy as I would like to?'

Would you agree that there's a huge difference between not feeling ill- maybe having just enough energy to get out of bed and go through the motions of work, family and social life, but never really feeling full of the joys of spring, compared with feeling great? That's feeling alive! Feeling full of energy. It's that 'Joi de Vivre' when we awaken feeling energised, vibrant, with a big smile on our face, after a deep, unbroken refreshing nights sleep. When we awaken feeling excited about our day ahead, looking forward to all the opportunities and adventures that each new day can bring. When we have the knowledge that we are physically and emotionally equipped and capable of dealing with anything and everything that life may offer us in a calm, relaxed, positive and confident manner. Well, I know which option I'm going for and you don't need me to tell you which one that is! Can you think of any conceivable reason why every single human in the entire universe wouldn't want that either? I really do not think that I can!

Perhaps this is a bit of a 'self-help' book after all!

## SO, WHAT ARE YOU LETTING YOURSELF IN FOR?

Now you have taken the plunge (excuse the pun) and bought this book, you are letting yourself in for some potentially life changing information. I say 'potentially' because in order for it to actually be life changing, you will need to not only read this book, but also DO it and LIVE it! If you only read this information without acting on it, then what's the point in reading it in the first place? I hope this book will be one of the most important books you ever read. If you really do put it all into practice and incorporate it into your everyday life

becoming more hydrated is the foundation upon which better health and happiness can be built.

My aim is to help you to understand why we all need to hydrate and drink *Water* and to give you a flexible guide as to how to do it, alongside an idea of the positive consequences of hydrating, together with some fascinating facts about the amazing substance we call *Water* along the way.

For all this to be successful for you, it's really important that you enjoy reading the following pages. This is not nor needs to be a dry biology or medical text book. (Apologies to all you Biologists and Medics out there!) It's also important that the changes you make within your lifestyle are practical, sustainable, easily made and fun, with the knowledge behind it all so you know quite clearly why you are doing it and that you want to do it all in order to enjoy feeling healthier and happier.

until *Water* and hydration become a high priority each day, you will reap the benefits and enjoy feeling and experiencing yourself hydrating. Like the leaves of a dry, wilted plant coming back to life and being restored to plump succulence once more! Like evolving from a prune into a plum. Sounds encouraging?

I'm not promising you that by drinking more *Water* and hydrating more that you will suddenly experience the 'Joi de Vivre' mentioned earlier. It's very likely that for most of us, there are a few more changes that need to be made! What I am saying, which I truly believe, is that

# 2

## INTRODUCING THE ELIXIR OF LIFE

*Please step further inside ...to the inner sanctum ...and let's get down to the nitty gritty.*

*Water* ...the source of all human life as we know it. It is the key to our health and the health of our planet, Mother Earth. What exactly is it?

*Water* is the most incredibly mysterious and special substance known to mankind. It sounds rather outlandish to say that it is living, but it is! Every little drop of *Water* is a microcosm of the outer Universe.

We are all taught in school that *Water* is made from two Hydrogen atoms and one Oxygen atom. Perhaps you remember the picture of one *Water* molecule looking like Mickey Mouse's head? A *Water* molecule is a simple formula, but the structure of *Water* is far from simple. $H_2O$ is really just the foundation of *Water*, because it gathers other substances along its way, like minerals in mineral *Water*. The chemical bonds that hold *Water* together are very weak, so they snap and change and reassemble millions of times per second, which allows it to respond to its environment and lets it remember its experiences, which of course, is how homeopathy is so effective.

On its own, it is totally colourless, tasteless and has no smell.

It is said that there are no two snowflakes alike in the entire universe, but how's this for an amazing fact? If we melted a snowflake and then refroze it under the same conditions, it would recreate the identical pattern of the original snowflake.

I hope you are now just beginning to realise (if you didn't already know) that there really is something uniquely special about *Water*. The chemical that we call *Water* is completely and utterly unique.

When we really think about it, the only reason that we can live on the Earth is because we have *Water* here. The Earth is very special in where it is situated. If we were much nearer the Sun, the Earth would be too hot and the *Water* would vaporise. If we were much further away from the Sun, then the Earth would be too cold and the *Water* would freeze into ice. As a result we are perfectly positioned to be able to have *Water* in all three states and to support life.

Mother Earth has rivers, streams and babbling brooks flowing through her to the seas and oceans. The *Water* evaporates, passes over the land as clouds, returns as rain which then falls onto the land, filters through the soil and rocks and continues flowing and circulating through and around our globe constantly. We can draw comparisons with ourselves as we breathe out *Water* vapour in our breath, then take *Water* into ourselves. This ends up, amongst other places, in our blood (which ideally is 85% *Water*) flowing through our arteries, veins and capillaries in an incredibly organised way to our cells, lungs and heart, constantly circulating. I find it fascinating to realise that we are a reflection of the world we live in.

Another interesting point is to consider that most scientists have thought for a long time that there is a finite amount of *Water* on and around our planet. I wonder if this is true? Could there be a bigger picture? Certainly *Water* is constantly changing its state from solid to liquid to gas depending on its environment. *Water* also constantly passes through people and animals. We perhaps don't like to think about it, but this has been happening since the beginning of time and so is completely and perfectly natural. When *Water* leaves us, for example, in our urine or in our perspiration, where do we think it goes to? Does it simply disappear? No, it circulates.

There are also other, less widely known theories and research which now throw up different possible scenarios.

Recent research seems to show that Black Holes actually produce *Water*.

Another idea I would like to include here is awesome. This one fits with the microcosm being reflected in the macrocosm. This is when we see that everything in the universe is a reflection of everything else on every level. To make this a little clearer, let's think of the example of how electrons orbit the nucleus of the atoms we are made of in a similar way to how the planets move around in the Universe.

I am going to challenge your paradigm of *Water* very strongly now, so are you sitting down and ready for this idea? Great, I knew you would be as open minded to new ideas as I am!

Well, apparently, satellite photographs often show black spots. In the past, these have often been thought to be comets. What has been suggested is that these comets are actually spheres of ice which travel through outer space to Earth. They

melt and evaporate with the sun's heat, then the *Water* vapour passes into our atmosphere and then falls to the ground as rain or even as snow.

Now the next bit of this idea. Our liver cleans our blood. Fact. Every drop of our blood passes through our liver every 3 or so minutes. Another fact. Our blood consists predominantly of *Water*. A further fact.

Thinking again about the microcosm being reflected in the macrocosm, what if Mother Earth is the liver of the universe? What if *Water* comes to our Earth to be cleaned and purified by flowing through the Earth and also by passing through people and animals before moving on?

It is feasible because if we, as individuals, need a constant circulation of *Water* through us, then maybe our universe needs this too. Food for thought. If this happens to be true, then what a responsibility we have!

*Water* is one 'thing' that connects us all as we all share it. Just think, the *Water* inside you today may have been in Barrack Obama or the Pope last week! It may be inside Queen Elizabeth of England or your next door neighbour's pet goldfish next week! We have possibly all shared *Water* with Jesus Christ and Ghandi. What do you think of that?

Remember, because it's so interesting; *Water* is the only chemical that can exist on Earth in all three states simultaneously!

# 3

## WHY IS WATER IMPORTANT?

To keep it all very simple, let's just think about what we are made of. When we really get down to basics, we are predominantly made of, guess what? Yes, you guessed it...*Water*! So, if Mother Nature has made us to be largely *Water*, then it stands to reason that it is rather important!

## HOW MUCH OF US IS WATER?

If we are talking about the ideal scenario then our blood is made of about 85-90% *Water*. Our lymph is made up of a similar amount of *Water*. (N.B. Our lymphatic system is part of our circulatory system, made up of lymphatic vessels that carry a clear fluid called lymph, which comes from the Latin word *lympha* meaning '*Water* goddess' directionally towards the heart.) This helps us to understand that everything is moved around our body in *Water*. Our bones are at their optimum health when they are around 40% *Water*. Even our tooth enamel is 1-2% *Water*. A full term baby in the womb is approximately 97% *Water*!

Every part of our body, including our blood, lymph and bones is made up exclusively of little cells. Depending on which book you read, between 50 to 100 trillion of them, so quite a few. Each one of these cells wants to be around 70% *Water*. The cells in our brain and spinal cord, which is called our Central Nervous System, function best when they are more like 85% *Water*. However, I doubt that any of us reading this book in this day and age is even approaching these percentages because there are so many things which de-hydrate us, as we shall be finding out!

## LET ME TELL YOU A LITTLE BIT MORE ABOUT OUR CELLS... BECAUSE THEY ARE US!

We have loads of different types of cells and they combine to make our tissues, which in turn make organs, which join to make systems, which form our whole body/mind. I use the term body/mind to show that our physical, emotional and mental states are completely intertwined rather than separate entities. Everything works together and nothing works in isolation, which is why it seems ludicrous to me to have a skin specialist or a heart specialist as our whole being is like a finely tuned orchestra.

It amazed me the first time I heard my teacher saying that every one of our cells is intelligent – or that every one of our 75 or so trillion cells knows exactly what to do. Just consider this – every second of every day each one of your cells is carrying out hundreds of processes in a beautifully organised way. On a conscious level, do you realise? No, of course not! Do we ever give it much thought? Probably not, but if I could take you down to the level of one of your cells at this very moment, you may start thinking about yourself very differently. You might not carry on seeing yourself as one big Samantha or Sonny, Jessica or James, because you would see yourself as an amazing, bustling community of cells all sending messages, 'talking' to each other, communicating constantly through electricity, through light and *yes, through Water*. Wow! What a vision that is.

Every one of our cells is a little miniature of us. It sounds a little unusual to say that 'we are our cells,' but we really are! We live in every one of them. We don't just live in our heads and walk around cut off from the rest of our body. On the contrary, whatever is going on in our cells is reflected in the whole of us. By that I mean exactly what I have said. If we are scared or anxious, then we have scared, anxious cells. If we feel cut off and isolated, then our cells are cut off and isolated. This is simply because each cell is a reflection of the whole of us. To use the jargon, our cells are the microcosm, reflected in the macrocosm.

This is a fascinating and exciting topic, because we are talking about you and me ...and what is our favourite subject?

So if we are our cells and each one of our cells is us, then it makes complete sense to learn how we can take care of each one of them as lovingly and diligently as possible, in order to take care of our big self. Are you beginning to see, hear, feel and understand why we need *Water*? Hope so!

# 4

## DEHYDRATION – LOSING THE ELIXIR

It's fair to say that dehydration is involved in every single negative issue, be it physical, emotional or mental. It would be impossible to experience any of the following and not have some level of dehydration:

Acid Reflux, Acne, ADHD, Allergies, Alzheimer's, Anxiety, Arthritis, Asthma, and that's naming only a few starting with the letter 'A'!

To continue off the top of my head... Constipation, Chronic Pain, Dry Skin, Headaches, Migraines, Chronic Back Issues, Scanty Periods, Poor Short Term Memory, Poor Concentration Levels, all Cancers, Depression, Infertility, Dyslexia, Eczema, Endometriosis, Gout, Fibromyalgia, IBS etc. The list is pretty much endless!

## HOW DO WE BECOME DEHYDRATED?

Let us think about the ways that we lose *Water* from our bodies every single day. Have you ever given it that much thought?

1. Well, there is the obvious way through weeing! Let's give it its Sunday name, which is *Urination*. The colour of our wee is a good indication of how hydrated (or not!) we are. We are aiming for it to be generally clear throughout the day. The first *Water* we pass in the morning may be light yellow if we have slept right through the night, but after that we are looking for it to be almost transparent. If it is dark yellow or orange and smells strong, then it is very concentrated, showing that our kidneys are conserving as much *Water* as possible and that we are deeply dehydrated.

The amount of *Water* we pass is going to vary depending on how much we take in through both fluids and foods, and whether that *Water* is able to be held in the body and flow freely into our cells, or whether we are like a dry hanging basket! (i.e. the *Water* pours straight through.) This can also be one of the consequences of beginning to drink more *Water*, which we chat about later. Basically, it is therefore possible to drink plenty of *Water* and still be dehydrated; *Water* alone is not the whole picture, so there is more to learn, but drinking *Water* is still fundamental to everything else.

2. We lose *Water* through our bowel movements. Sunday name being *Defacation*. Constipation is a clear sign of dehydration. It means that our body is absorbing back every drop of moisture that it possibly can from our waste, making our poo drier, more compacted and harder, often ending up like sheep droppings. What do you think may be a definition of the ideal bowel movement? Well, how about 'Twice round the toilet bowl, conker coloured, formed, starts to break up immediately it hits the *Water* in the toilet and no need to use toilet paper.' I wonder how many of us have bowel movements like that? Something to aim for!

At the other end of the scale, loose, *Watery* bowel movements, or full on diarrhoea will lose much more *Water*. Chronic diarrhoea is said to be a deeper form of constipation, because by this situation, the bowel may have some inflammation going on and the bowel may be trying to get the waste out as quickly as possible.

3. We also lose *Water* through our skin – Sunday name being *Perspiration*. What's the old saying? 'Horses sweat, Men perspire and Ladies glow.' Well, whatever! We all lose *Water* through our skin, which is our biggest organ, and the perspiration carries *Water* soluble toxicity with it, so it is a very good thing. Of course it is neither comfortable nor desirable to perspire excessively. The amount we lose through our skin will vary of course, depending on the amount we perspire. This will increase with exercise, hot weather, stress, and on occasions if we have a fever.

4. Have you ever realised that we breathe out *Water* vapour? Sunday name being *Respiration*! You don't believe me? Well, breathe out on some cold glass or a mirror and see it condense into *Water*. Again, the amount we lose every day through breathing will vary. It will increase when we breathe more deeply with exercise for example, or when we are stressed and breathe more shallowly and faster.

Other ways we lose *Water*, although not necessarily every day include:

5. We ladies lose *Water* through the blood we lose every month with our periods. Sunday name being *Menstruation*.

6. Crying – *Lacrimation*.

7. Breast feeding – *Lactation*.

8. Injuries including burns and blood loss.

9. Acute episodes including vomiting and diarrhoea.

These last few examples are not really what I want to focus on. I merely wish to bring your awareness to other ways we lose *Water* at different times, and consequently, in these cases, our need for hydration will be even greater than usual.

The point I really want to make here very clearly, is that we all lose a substantial amount of *Water* every single day through natural processes.

Thinking about it in this way makes us realise quite shockingly, that every single day we are taking in less *Water* than we lose, we are getting more and more and more dehydrated.

*Dear Optimist, Pessimist & Realist,*

*While you guys were busy arguing about the glass of Water, I drank it!*

*Sincerely,*
*The Opportunist.*

The extent of our dehydration is much deeper than we have touched on so far.

I believe it is important that we understand the enormity of the dehydration problem going on in this day and age, as it is the start of every single illness. Luckily, we have good news in terms of being able to address it all with some solutions!

What could be worse than not drinking any *Water*? Drinking substances that make us lose even more *Water* than the *Water* that is in them? What could these substances be?

Do you know what the second largest industry in the world is? The coffee revolution. What's the first you may be wondering? It is the petrochemical industry. (That's purely for interest as hopefully none of us are drinking petrol!)

Would you believe that around 1.6 billion cups of coffee are drunk worldwide every day? That's a heck of a lot! But because coffee is made from *Water*, why does drinking it make us lose *Water*?

The ingredient in coffee that gives us that 'boost' is caffeine. When we drink any caffeinated drink, and this includes fizzy drinks, hot chocolate, tea, (even green tea contains small amounts of caffeine), our bodies need to use a lot of *Water* to get rid of the caffeine. When we drink the caffeine, it causes our adrenal glands, which sit on top of our kidneys, to release certain substances called hormones – and the adrenals make our stress hormones. These cause our bodies to secrete an emergency supply of sugar into our bloodstream, which gives us that 'boost' or 'kick-start'. To get rid of the caffeine from the blood, the body is forced to use *Water*. So, for every caffeinated beverage we drink, we use several cups of *Water* to deal with the chaos. This consequently results in more dehydration. The drying effect of the caffeine in soft drinks is a good enough reason not to drink them, but there are plenty more detrimental reasons not to drink them including the vast amount of refined sugar they contain, which is another story about more internal stress. Given that in the UK the amount of soft drinks we pour down our necks has more than doubled since 1985 — from around 10 gallons to 25 gallons per person per year, this is scary. Last year, we apparently downed a whopping amount of over 14 million litres of soft drinks. How dehydrating is that?

Maybe you are a tea drinker. If so, you're in good company, as it's thought that there are over 4 million cups of tea drunk each day in the UK. Not quite as dehydrating as coffee, but it's not far behind.

Herbal teas are a different kettle of fish, provided they contain no caffeine, so it's a great idea to foray into the herbal varieties. There are so many to try, from chamomile to nettle to peppermint to ginger to red bush to fruity ones… You may already enjoy them and certainly with perseverance you may get to love some of them.

'So, what about de-caffeinated coffee and tea then?' I hear you asking. Well, of course they haven't got as much caffeine so will therefore be less dehydrating, but do remember that de-caff doesn't mean no-caff. Also, the chemicals often used in the de-caffeinating process can be just as detrimental as the caffeine albeit in different ways, so it's certainly not a permanent solution. Going on to de-caffeinated drinks can be a good stepping stone in the process of cutting down with a view to cutting caffeine out completely and is certainly a move in the right direction. There are a few coffee substitutes on the market mainly made from ingredients such as acorns, chicory and barley that, although not identical to coffee, at least have that bitter taste that so many coffee drinkers enjoy.

Then there's alcohol that some of us tipple regularly. Even if we only consider beer, it's documented that over 27 million pints are sold in the UK every day. Crikey, that's a good few slurps. Is alcohol also causing us to lose more *Water*? You bet it is!

Getting the picture a little bit more? Of course you are…

*…And what do you think is the most dehydrating thing of all?*

## IT'S TIME TO CONSIDER THE 'S' WORD

Mmmmmnn, the 'S' word. What am I talking about? Sugar? Sweeties? Shopping? None of these...

I want to have a chat about *STRESS* – the most dehydrating thing of all.

Have you come across the word 'STRESS' in your neck of the woods? I'm sure you have. Everyone seems to talk about being stressed these days, even children. It's so common for people to be off work with 'stress', so common to hear the word here, there and everywhere, so I suppose it means different things to different people. We may be stressed because we have too much work to do, because we haven't enough money to pay our mortgage, or because we are being bullied at work – all unpleasant things going on. Our cells, however, are not really too bothered about all that. Our cells will be stressed because they are not getting enough *Water*.

Let's think about stress in four different categories:

Acute, Chronic, Internal and External.

How do they differ?

## ACUTE STRESS

This is something that is intense but short-lived. Nature has provided us with wonderful ways to deal with acute stress.

If we think back to caveman or cavewoman days, when our ancestors were being sized up by hungry looking wild animals, their 'Fight, Flight or Freeze' mechanism would kick in. They needed to either run away and get out of danger quickly or stay and fight the animal! Hopefully, in these particular scenarios, the 'freeze' option wasn't chosen! 'Fight, Flight or Freeze' is our ancient survival mechanism that has kept humans alive over the centuries and continues to be activated instantaneously whenever we encounter a situation that we perceive as threatening.

Umpteen things happen in our bodies to create extra strength and energy to allow us to deal with whatever situation we have found ourselves in ...and get out alive! We will all have experienced the usual symptoms at some time or other

I'm sure, which include:

1. Heart beating quicker.

2. Breathing becoming shallower and faster in our upper chest. Losing more *Water* vapour.

3. The urge to go to the loo, either to pass *Water* or to open our bowels. This causes us to lose *Water* and consequently makes us lighter, so if we were being chased by a sabre-toothed tiger, we would be able to run faster and stay alive. Nature is wonderful.

4. Perspiring more. Again, more *Water* loss.

5. Production of the hormone adrenaline which causes us to secrete an emergency supply of sugar into our bloodstream.

6. Blood supply to our frontal cortex in our brain is restricted, causing us to simply react, rather than think.

7. The fluids in our bodies are moved around to where the priorities are at that moment in time, causing a dry mouth.

We can begin to see that losing *Water* from different areas of the body is made much more difficult if there is a *Water* shortage and there are umpteen more processes that go on in our bodies to help us.

We can clearly see therefore, as I have indicated, that 'Fight, Flight or Freeze', our ancient survival mechanism, causes us to lose *Water*!

In this day and age, we are unlikely to be approached by a hungry looking sabre-toothed tiger, but we may have a double decker bus hurtling down the road at us! Our bodies miraculously create extra strength and energy by all the ways listed above, and more, to allow us to get out of the situation fast. Then, when that situation is over and done with, our bodies recover and we are back to square one. On the whole, we are geared up to deal with acute stresses, which are short lived and we don't need to be overly concerned about their dehydrating effects.

## CHRONIC STRESS

This is another matter. Chronic stress is when we have those ongoing, day in, day out stresses that seem to be with us constantly. It creates the same symptoms as acute stresses, but generally less intense. It stands to reason though, that even whilst being milder, if they are going on continually as in chronic stress, they are extremely dehydrating.

Then we see a vicious circle as the stress causes dehydration, which causes more internal stress, which causes more dehydration ad infinitum. Moving on...

## EXTERNAL STRESS

External stresses include some of the scenarios we have already mentioned, like our worries about finances, relationships and work, all of which are outside of us. We can internalise these as we think about them and of course, our thoughts and emotions also contribute to internal stress, but the initial source of those particular stresses tend to be outside of us. Many of these external stresses are not within our control, as they often involve the actions of other people, and much as we would sometimes like other people to be different or act differently, we cannot control them. Yet how many of us spend so much time, effort and angst trying to change things that we are not in control of? And how stressful is that?

My humble suggestion is, to try to let go of the need to change the things that are not ours to change.

Should we just take a moment to consider what we, as individual human beings are in control of?

After due consideration I hope you will agree that we are in control of our own thoughts (we may not always think we are, but we are) therefore, indirectly, our feelings (as these are affected by how we think) and also what we do (which covers a multitude). What else are we in control of? Come on, think! What else?

Interestingly, the truth of it is that we are in control of absolutely nothing else!

This is worth really mulling over in our minds; even deliberating, cogitating and digesting, as Lloyd Grossman used to say, and making a huge effort to stop trying to change things that we as individuals cannot change. Of course this is not always an easy thing to do, but if we can try and work towards achieving it more and more, without question it will feel a huge relief and consequently reduce our stress and therefore will be less dehydrating!

Bear in mind that within the category of being in control of what we 'do' falls drinking adequate amounts of *Water* and reducing the dehydrating substances we consume. Read on…

## INTERNAL STRESSES

Internal stresses, on the other hand, are within our control. These are created by things like:

1. All the stimulants we ingest, such as coffee, tea, sugar, chocolate, alcohol, drugs and cigarettes.

2. Not having all the nutrients we need in order to make all our bits and pieces like hormones, enzymes, our hair, skin, tissues to name but a few.

3. An inability to get rid of our 'waste'. This is when our routes of elimination

are sluggish and congested, as in the case of being constipated.

4. Thoughts. Our thoughts can create a huge amount of internal stress. Think about the language we sometimes use when speaking to ourselves: "I'm so stupid. Why did I do that? I'm never going to be good enough. I'm so thick and clumsy." Very stressful for us when we think these kinds of thoughts as every thought we think is communicated to every cell in our bodies at the speed of light!

We are extremely good at making an 'Acute' stress become a 'Chronic' one by our thoughts. We do this by thinking, 'What if.....' and creating awful scenarios in our mind. This perpetuates the stress.

5. Emotions. Bottling up our emotions is a great way of contributing to inner stress, and how great are we at doing that? The study of emotions is a whole subject in itself. Years ago, I didn't realise how completely interconnected our physical, emotional and mental state is. We now know that our emotions have a physical base. We create physical molecules of emotion, so every single feeling we experience has to have the biochemistry to support it! If, therefore, we do not allow ourselves to express an emotion, but simply push it to the back of our mind and swallow down those tears or zip up our lips and walk away seething, what the heck do we expect happens to them? Do they disappear? No, we carry the resonance and vibration of those emotions in our body forever until we are prepared to process it. In order to let go of these emotions from our body, as well as expressing an emotion by, for example, crying and talking, we also need to be able to dissolve the physical molecules of emotion using enzymes and essential fatty acids. It is said that we can create more toxicity from our thoughts and bottled up emotions than we ever could from our food. Something to ponder!

6. Not having enough *Water*. Surprise surprise!! In my opinion, this has to be one of the biggest internal stresses, and please remember that it becomes a vicious circle as dehydration causes internal stress which causes more dehydration which causes more stress.

In a nutshell, *STRESS* is the most dehydrating thing of all. We are not too concerned about acute or external – it's the chronic, internal stresses we need to work on, because we can. The more we reduce our internal stress, then the better equipped we are to deal with our external stresses. We will be able to think more clearly and be able to make more beneficial decisions as we will be accessing our frontal cortex in our brain.

# 5

## GAINING THE ELIXIR

We have talked about the many ways in which we lose *Water*, so now let us consider the ways we gain it.

By drinking it. This would seem fairly obvious, but if the *Water* has anything in it, be it a tea bag or juice, then our bodies treat it very differently from plain, still, clean *Water*.

From our food. This is not rocket science to realise that if we are eating a diet that consists of things like:

**Breakfast:** toast/cereal/fry-up.
**Mid-morning:** coffee/tea/biscuit/chocolate.
**Lunch:** sandwich/pie/crisps.
**Mid-afternoon:** tea/coffee/cake.
**Evening meal:** pasta/pizza/processed ready meals/takeaways.

...then clearly there is little *Water* being gained from the above way of eating.

On the other hand, if we are consuming good amounts of fruit and vegetables, then it is easy to see that we are gaining *Water* from our food.

The *Water* in the cells of raw fruits and vegetables is called 'structured' *Water* and is extremely beneficial for us.

Perhaps surprisingly, short-grain brown rice, when soaked and cooked slowly in large amounts of *Water*, is a wonderfully hydrating food to eat. The ratio of *Water* to rice that it holds is approximately 75:25. This also happens to be a similar ratio of *Water* to solid in our bodies and *Water* to land on Mother Earth!

As a by-product of our metabolism, we produce a small amount of *Water* too. Perhaps this is Mother Nature's real lifesaver.

We also breathe in *Water* vapour and absorb *Water* through our skin when bathing, but not in significant amounts to be able to rely on instead of drinking it!

The picture starts to become much clearer. If we are not drinking enough *Water* to bridge the gap between the amount of *Water* we lose compared to the amount of *Water* we take in, then every day there will be a shortfall and every single day we are getting that bit more dehydrated. Now we have an understanding about how we can become dehydrated.

# 6

DROUGHT MANAGEMENT

*If our cells want to be 70% Water, as we have stated, what happens when they are not getting enough Water?*

This is an interesting question which has fascinating answers, so let us get to grips with this predicament.

It is wonderful to realise that our bodies never make a mistake. This is not always easy to believe, but the Naturopathic philosophy is based on this principle. We are now going to see how amazingly our bodies respond to dehydration.

If our cells lose too much *Water*, there is no two ways about it – they will die. When our body recognises that there is a drought going on inside, it takes action to prevent our cells from dying. We call this going on 'Dehydration Alert.' We produce more cholesterol. You may be thinking that cholesterol is a bad guy. Well, cholesterol has been given such a bad press over the years, but if we believe that our bodies never make a mistake, then if we are producing excess cholesterol, we are doing it for a good reason! Although this may not be the only reason that we make excess cholesterol, one reason is to deposit it in our cell membranes like putty, to stop our cells from losing too much *Water*. Isn't this a genius idea to protect our cells from the effects of dehydration? The concern about this, though, is that we are now beginning to move away from a lovely internal environment where we have movement and flow in the body, towards stagnancy and stuckness, which manifests on every level. Ask yourself, 'Am I able to go with the flow or do I feel stuck and stagnant in my life?' Another problem with this is that over time, our cell membrane gets more and more enmeshed with cholesterol as dehydration gets deeper and deeper, until our cell membrane is much denser and more rigid, resulting in our cell being colder and darker because the light cannot pass through the membrane. This can eventually result in the cell being cut off and isolated from the other cells around it – again manifest on every level. Clearly, therefore, we do not want to be blasé about being dehydrated, and we do not want our body to need to resort to this protective action!

We could discuss many scenarios resulting from having a shortage of *Water*, but I don't want this to be a science book, so let's just consider one other situation; eating! I hope you will find this interesting, because you eat, we all eat! We rarely stop eating!

As soon as we start to think about food, or smell it, or see it or hear something that reminds us of it, our digestive system starts to prepare for the food that is to come by producing digestive juices. What are these

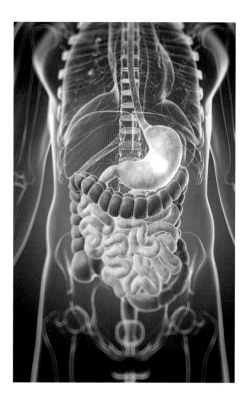

digestive juices predominantly made of? Yes, you've guessed it, *Water*. When we put our food in our mouth and chew, the idea is to coat the food with the saliva containing the digestive enzymes so that the chewed up food starts to be digested even before it is swallowed. Would you say that this rarely happens because so many people hardly chew? Let's have a bit of fun watching our nearest and dearest and see how many times they chew before swallowing! Let's notice ourselves too. Our swallowed food then moves down our oesophagus into our stomach. This is a bit like a washing machine. It churns and mixes and mulches, pouring more *Water* onto the chewed up food to break it down more. Good old $H_2O$ to the rescue again! The less well-chewed the food, the more *Water* is needed to be poured on it. The process of breaking down a chemical compound into two or more simpler compounds by reacting with *Water* is called hydrolysis. Proteins, fats, and complex carbohydrates in our food are broken down in our digestive tract by hydrolysis. After leaving the stomach, we then have to push this through 20-odd feet of small intestine, which is no mean feat, never mind considering the copious amounts of a *Watery* bicarbonate solution that the pancreas produces to neutralise the incredibly acidic and corrosive gloop that moves from the stomach into the duodenum. Is it any wonder that there are so many duodenal ulcers around? Are we beginning to realise the importance of *Water* in digesting our food?

The dilemma for our body is that as soon as we eat something, our digestion needs to become a top priority. We really must attend to the food passing through us. We cannot simply allow it to stagnate and decompose inside us! That doesn't bear thinking about. What is going to happen, though, if we haven't got any spare *Water* to deal with what we have just eaten? Think of a really dry, stodgy meal like pizza and chips. These foods need a lot of *Water* to be able to deal with them. What are we going to do if we are already deeply dehydrated? We will probably feel extremely thirsty half way through eating, which by that time is too late, as by drinking with food, we are diluting our digestive juices, which messes up our digestion. Can you think of anything else we can do?

Fortunately, our bodies are incredible. They are amazingly resourceful. We have a fabulously efficient way of prioritising where our *Water* needs to be at any point in time, so if we haven't got enough spare *Water* to deal with digesting the food we have just eaten, we will divert it from somewhere else. How clever! However, as wonderful as this system is, do we really want to rely on this mechanism to rescue us? Do we really want to take *Water* from the cells in other parts of our body and prevent the important jobs that are being carried out there? As wonderful as we are at 'drought management' we really do not want to remain in a situation where we need to resort to this on a regular basis! It will simply contribute to regular internal stress and more and more dehydration.

# 7

following morning if the situation hasn't changed? Extremely panicky now? Quite literally petrified because you know that if you don't get some *Water* soon, you will certainly die!

That's exactly how our cells feel when they know that they aren't getting enough *Water*! They know that they can simply dehydrate and dehydrate until death.

Whether we live in Australia, America or Austria; Woking, Wolverhampton or Wigan; Bristol, Bradford or Blairgowrie; Holyhead, Huddersfield or Hove; if we are fortunate, we are likely to be surrounded by *Water* with taps, springs, bottles and filters available everywhere. But if we are not drinking the stuff and, even worse, if we are drinking all the other stuff that makes us *lose Water*, then as far as our cells are concerned, we may as well be stuck in the middle of the desert because our cells are suffering a drought!

Going back to the desert scenario, if a glass of *Water* mysteriously appeared every hour for you to drink, you may find that after a while you start to feel somewhat reassured that you are getting a regular supply of *Water*. This may allow you to begin to relax about it to a certain extent.

Similarly, as our cells begin to receive *Water* regularly and consistently, they

## EMOTIONS

Let's also consider how our cells start to feel when they realise that they are not getting enough *Water*. Also remember that we are our cells, so our cells, being us, will experience emotions.

Close your eyes and imagine this scenario for a moment. You are driving through the desert, a long way from civilisation when your jeep breaks down. You have only one bottle of *Water* left as you were expecting to reach the next oasis before sunset. Once you have finished that bottle, how are you likely to feel about the fact that you have no more *Water*? Concerned? Worried? Anxious? Several hours pass. You are perspiring, breathing out, stressing, doing all the things that lose *Water*. How are you feeling now? Very concerned? Very worried? Very anxious? Maybe a bit panicky now? What about the

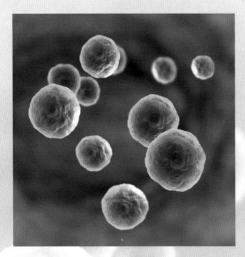

can stop feeling anxious about dying from being in a drought. As our cells experience reassurance, with a regular supply of *Water*, we can also start to move away from that awful free floating anxiety, fear and panic.

We, as the whole person, can of course experience worry, anxiety, fear and panic about a whole range of scenarios – this fits in with the external stress we talked about a few moments ago. Remember though, that our cells are really not overly bothered about our external stresses like our bank account, our deadlines at work etc, they simply want a regular supply of *Water*. Also remember that the less internal stress we have, then the more we can think clearly and feel so much more capable of dealing with those external goings on!

# 8

## NATURAL THIRST

*"But I never feel thirsty, so I obviously don't need to drink any more Water," you may say. Is this true? Why is it that many of us never feel thirsty for Water?*

Well let's consider the following. Does it sound familiar?

We get some sort of message from our body-mind saying, 'Please can I have some *Water*?'

What do many of us do?

We have a cup of tea or coffee or a glass of some sort of fizzy drink – all substances that cause us to lose more *Water*. Consequently, our body-mind thinks, 'Well that's rather funny, because I asked for some *Water* and I've been given something that makes me lose *Water*!' (Remember that tea, coffee, sodas etc are all diuretics, which means they are particularly stressful to the body-mind that the end result is *Water* loss, even though we are getting the fluid initially as we drink it! Repetition is the mother of skill ...although I'll not tell you again!)

Consequently, we often get another similar message shortly afterwards, asking for *Water*, but often we mistake that by thinking, 'I can't be thirsty because I've just had a drink. I must be hungry, so I'll have something to eat.' Because of this process, many of us mistake our thirst signals for hunger signals, and probably have done for years.

Over a period of time, our body-mind stops bothering to ask for *Water* when requests are constantly ignored, resulting in our 'Natural Thirst Mechanism' shutting down.

In my experience, once we begin drinking more plain, still, clean *Water*, we reactivate our natural thirst and begin to become thirstier. If we are not aware that this will happen, it can seem rather odd, because we are now drinking more *Water* but getting thirstier! Actually, this is exactly what we want to happen and shows us just how quickly our body-mind can respond. Our aim is to gradually and steadily increase our *Water* intake over a period of time, maybe over a month or two up to around two litres or four pints per day. Once we get to this amount and

maintain it for a couple of weeks, our natural thirst will generally be kick-started. When this happens, the idea is to listen to our body and it will tell us what we need. Once we establish our natural thirst, this enables us to easily sustain drinking adequate amounts of *Water*, because we want it. This makes it easy and therefore successful.

*One of the very best things we can ever do for our children is to help them to activate their natural thirst for Water* and ensure there's always a supply of clean, fresh, still *Water* available, rather than the stimulants which ultimately cause *Water* loss. I always think a bit of bribery is the best way with children. It's absolutely no good being high-handed and authoritarian and telling them to drink *Water* when they say they want a fizzy drink instead. How about making it fun and rewarding them afterwards. Drink a glass together every hour. Let them have a very special glass or drinking beaker that is reserved purely for *Water*. Praise them for drinking it rather than criticising them for not drinking it. Explain to them about their cells and the fact that they are made of cells and their cells need *Water* to be happy. With some gentle encouragement and perseverance alongside setting the example ourselves, our children will respond. Once their natural thirst is established, our children will want to continue drinking *Water*. This is the result we are aiming for.

This is a fairly simple and theoretically easy process, but stop for just a moment and consider the enormity of what achieving it could mean. Imagine our youngsters growing up drinking adequate amounts of *Water*, having their natural thirst for *Water* activated from a very early age. What would be the benefits to mankind of this generation being more hydrated? Being able to think more clearly? Being less motivated by anxiety and more by knowing where they want to go and what they want to do? Envisage this generation becoming parents and passing on the hydration message, at conception and through pregnancy. What dis-eases could this prevent? What suffering could this reduce? If we are predominantly made of *Water* and all messages are passed through the body in *Water*, then surely hydrating has to play a huge role not only in the correction of dis-ease, but also in the prevention of it in the first place.

Is this pie in the sky? No. It simply needs us all to take responsibility for encouraging and helping the children of the world to drink adequate amounts of plain, still, clean *Water*, and the best way to motivate them to cultivate this wonderful habit is to show by our own example. It needs to become the norm. It needs to be trendy. It needs to be cool.

Surely it's cool to be healthy, flexible, and energetic, clear headed and happy with glowing skin, bright eyes and a radiant smile?

# 9

*May I suggest that you have a go at the following and prove it to yourself. Please think of this as a flexible regime and aim for it very, very gradually.*

Try not to drink *Water* when you are eating. When *Water* and food are in the stomach together, the *Water* dilutes the digestive juices, interfering with the digestive process, potentially contributing to incompletely digested food moving from the stomach into the small intestine. When *Water* is consumed 30 minutes prior to food, it gives us available *Water* to deal with our digestion rather than having to scavenge it from other areas of our bodies like our brain. If we haven't got enough spare *Water* to deal with digesting our food, then we might have been about to remember something we have been trying to remember for ages, or about to have the most creative thought

we have ever had, but 'Oh No' the *Water* may be pulled away to hydrolyse our food. The *Water* also contributes to forming the mucosal lining of the stomach, which helps to protect it from the very strong acids in there. Another job is to thin our blood to prepare it for receiving more nutrients from our food. Can you imagine the chaos if our blood is already so thick and sludgy and then is forced to take in more substances because we have just eaten another meal? No wonder there is so much high blood pressure around.

It's a good idea to wait 60 minutes after food before having large amounts of *Water*, to enable our digestive system to function optimally.

The following regime is a reasonably sensible guideline to aim for, without being so rigid that we become stressed:

• One pint/500mls of *Water* on rising. Wait 30 minutes before breakfast.

• Glass (half a pint/250 mls) mid-morning.

• One pint/500mls 30 minutes before lunch.

• Glass (half a pint/250mls) mid-afternoon.

• One pint/500mls 30 minutes before evening meal.

• Glass (half a pint/250mls) during evening.

• Glass (half a pint/250mls) before bed.

The ideal temperature for our drinking *Water* is that of blood – a little warmer than room temperature. To achieve this if using a pint glass, pour three quarters full from the filter and top up with boiling *Water* from the kettle. If we drink *Water* that's very cold, it will tend to sit in the stomach until the body has warmed it up before absorbing it into the body. Likewise with hot *Water* – the body will cool it down first. Blood temperature *Water* is also nice and easy to drink ...find out for yourself!

### LET'S ALWAYS TAKE A BOTTLE OF WATER WITH US!

Drinking at regular intervals throughout the day is important. It would be far less beneficial to drink a very large amount all at once then nothing for hours on end. Remember, we want to reassure our body-minds that there is no drought going on. It's absolutely no good getting to bedtime and thinking, 'Oh heck! I haven't had any *Water* today yet,' and then downing four pints on the bounce.

Let's always take a bottle of *Water* with us wherever we go.

We will benefit from getting into the habit of always having a container of *Water* with us, wherever we may be... in the car, motorbike pannier, bicycle holder, on our desk at work, in our bag, sending our children off to school with some (and talking to school to encourage them to provide good quality *Water* for the children and to encourage them to drink during their lessons.)

We can drink too much *Water*. Never have more than one pint/500mls in any hour and set an upper limit of around 3-4 pints in any one day until we get to know ourselves very well. We can drink a little more if we are very stressed or doing lots of exercise and sweating. Other reasons to drink a little more may be when the weather is very hot or we are in a hot environment, when we are feverish or when symptoms like vomiting and diarrhoea are present, resulting in quite a lot of fluid loss.

*Please note* – that in the case of HEART FAILURE, WATER RETENTION, SWELLING or KIDNEY DISEASE, or if you have ANY cause for concern, it is extremely important to only increase *Water* consumption under supervision.

May I repeat myself one more time when I say that IT IS ALWAYS A GOOD IDEA TO MAKE ANY CHANGES TO OUR BODIES SLOWLY AND GRADUALLY!

### POSSIBLE CONSEQUENCES OF BEGINNING TO DRINK MORE WATER

Imagine what happens when we pour *Water* into a dry hanging basket. Yes, of course, it all goes straight through and pours out of the bottom. However, if we keep dripping the *Water* in and allow the soil to become moist, we can pour more *Water* into the basket and it will stay there much more easily. It's much the same with our bodies. Initially, when we first start our hydration regime, we often find that we need to visit the loo a lot more as though the *Water* is going straight in and straight out! Gradually, though, as in the analogy of the hanging basket, we find that as we begin to absorb the *Water* into our cells (which is where we want it to flow) and as our urine gets less acidic, helping our bladders to become stronger; the initial problem of needing to pass *Water* so frequently will begin to fade.

If needing to go to the loo too frequently is a real problem in the initial stages of starting to hydrate, then Linseed Tea can be very helpful (...that bit is later on, so either cheat and jump forward ...or be patient!)

I'm sure that it goes without saying that the long term consequences of drinking *Water* are amazingly wonderful. I simply want you to be aware of a possible initial need to visit the bathroom more frequently.

The benefits are endless, because starting to hydrate is the first step towards greater health and happiness, and every journey begins with the first step. Depending on your current level of hydration, you will all notice different changes of varying degrees and timescales. Fairly quickly you may notice the colour of your urine becoming lighter. Bowel movements may improve, especially if there has been chronic constipation. You may experience dry skin feeling and looking more moisturised from within. Thought processes are likely to become clearer and your energy may increase. I can't tell you just how important it is to persevere until you kick-start your natural thirst. Then you will have more awareness of how much *Water* you need each day. We are all completely unique, special individuals of all variety of shapes and sizes. We will all need varying amounts of *Water* daily. Some of us may find that we need two litres or more every day. Others of us, especially if we are consuming plenty of *Water*-rich fruit and vegetables and well-cooked short grain brown rice may need less. We need to realise that if we have started from a place of deep dehydration, then we need to be more extreme initially, without overdoing it (remember the guidelines about *changes needing to be made gently*

*and gradually*) and then as we hydrate and return to balance, we may require less *Water* daily to maintain the status quo.

In summary, our aim is to reassure the receptors in our colon that we are getting a regular, adequate supply of *Water*. This message will be passed on to our liver, which in Traditional Chinese Medicine is deemed to be the 'Planner' of our body. Our liver will then switch off 'dehydration alert' which will discontinue the production of extra cholesterol to plug up the cell membranes to prevent them from losing too much *Water* and dehydrating to death.

Let us always remember with awe and respect that our body-minds know exactly what to do. We all have an innate healing ability within us. We may not consciously know how to do it, but at another level we know it perfectly. Our job is simply to drink enough *Water*. Surely that's not such a big ask!? Putting it another way, to play our part in starting the ball rolling towards better health and happiness, we simply need to open our mouths, pour some *Water* in regularly and swallow. When we really stop to think about the massive rewards and benefits that we shall get in return, how easy is that?

# 10

up in the mountains, flowing over the rocks. Equally, this is nothing like the *Water* we find in a stagnant puddle yet we call it the same – *Water*! In parts of Scandinavia, they have many different words to describe snow because it is so important to them, and I feel that we need the same with *Water*. Whilst all *Water* pretty much looks the same, clearly it is not and the differing effects on our bodies and therefore on our health can be immense.

*Water* is like a living creature, responding to its environment. We've talked about living *Water*, so let's try to understand what that really means. In nature, *Water* constantly moves. Naturally, it doesn't flow in a straight line. It meanders, swirls and spirals as it flows. It creates vortexes. Even the steam coming off a hot drink spirals! Whilst flowing in a natural way, *Water* becomes more energised by the vortexes. Picture a beautiful babbling brook flowing through gorgeous woodland. The *Water*, like a living creature, frolicking along, whirling and twirling, racing and chasing, twisting and turning, dancing and prancing, splashing and crashing, gathering speed at times, slower at others, almost as though it is having fun, enjoying every second of its freedom. Listen and perhaps you can hear it giggling in the sunlight, laughing with infectious joy. This *Water* is becoming energised along its journey. This is the epitome of pure, clean, fresh, energised living *Water*.

## VARIETIES OF WATER AVAILABLE

*"What TYPE of Water should I drink?" is possibly going to be your first question, followed closely by, "I hope that tap Water is alright to drink, seeing as it is free of charge and easily available"...*

*Mmm... Another chinwag needed here...*

In the developed areas of the world we really do have plenty of choice as to the type of *Water* we can drink, yet how can it all be called *Water* when it is all very different?

I'm being serious when I say that I really do think that we need some different words in our vocabulary to describe *Water*, because the substance that comes out of our taps each day, sometimes smelling vaguely of bleach, is nothing like the substance that we find

In contrast, think about all the man-made pipes that force our municipal *Water* to flow in a straight line. No comparison!

Could it be that *Water* has a way of creating, losing and exchanging energy that we still don't fully understand and at present have no way of measuring? It would be arrogant to suggest that we know everything that there is to know about *Water* wouldn't it?!

It isn't a straightforward choice when it comes to deciding which type of *Water* to drink, as there are many kinds of *Water* available to us. Some options we have are:

• Tap *Water* straight from the tap.

• Tap *Water* that has been left to stand in a jug for several hours.

• Boiled Tap *Water* left to go cold.

• Bottled *Water*s... Mineral, Spring, Still, Sparkling, Flavoured, in Glass or Plastic Bottles.

• A whole minefield of Filters.

• Mechanisms to produce a vortex.

• Distilled *Water*.

• Rain *Water*.

• Treated with Ozone and Ultra Violet.

## TAP WATER

This is certainly not ideal, but let me make it perfectly clear that we are better drinking tap *Water* than not drinking *Water* at all. Please do not wait until you have researched or accessed the 'best' *Water* for you to drink before you start drinking some. Begin now! I clearly remember a student from years ago, who was such a perfectionist that she felt that she needed to research the 'perfect' *Water* before she could drink it and a couple of months down the line, in her eyes she still hadn't found the 'perfect' *Water* and in the meantime hadn't been drinking any which is clearly defeating the whole object.

You may remember learning in school about the process whereby *Water* evaporates, then passes as clouds over the land and falls as rain. This has the natural light from the sun beaming down on it, imprinting it with far infra-red energy. As the rain falls on the earth, it flows both over and through it, filtering through the layers of the land, which not only naturally cleanses and mineralises it but also energises it with the magnetic energy of the earth. *Water* is made to flow. The resulting *Water* bubbling out from Mother Earth was real, natural *Water*. It was clean, fresh, energised and alive! The clusters of the $H_2O$ molecules were small – only about three or four in each cluster, so in layman's terms it was almost like 'wetter' *Water* and this is more easily absorbed into our cells.

People in years gone by were lucky enough to have this beautiful, real, natural *Water*. Unfortunately, today our air is not quite as pure as it used to be. Consequently, the rain passes through air polluted with a variety of things including sulphuric acid hence the term 'acid rain.'

Before it comes through our taps, much of our *Water* is filtered in a man-made way and has chemicals put into it, like chlorine, to kill the bacteria. Clearly, for those of us who live in the more developed areas of the world, our tap *Water* is substantially better than 100 years ago when people died from drinking *Water* that was contaminated with all sorts of pollutants. However, if the chlorine is killing off the bacteria in the *Water*, what might it be doing to the helpful bacteria in our digestive systems? It is extremely clear that if we wish to drastically improve and maintain our health, then we need to cultivate the correct kind of bacteria in all areas of our gut. Something to consider. It's interesting to note that our lovely, friendly bowel flora can manufacture two thirds of our B Vitamins for us, Vitamin K and lots of other lovely stuff. Our bowel flora are our very best friends. And stress (have you come across this word?) gobbles up B Vitamins (as well as *Water*).

The other problem with chlorine is that it is highly volatile and easily joins with pollutants in the *Water* to produce substances called tri-halo-methanes. These are to be avoided.

We can take this further to question what happens when tap *Water* is heated and used in our showers and baths. The toxins evaporate, become airborne and are breathed in. Our bath and shower rooms essentially become gas chambers. There are also other routes into our bodies such as the absorption through our skin whilst we carry out our ablutions. It is said that we can potentially breathe in as many pollutants during a short hot shower as we would get from drinking around four litres of polluted *Water*!

It therefore makes complete sense to not only choose better quality *Water* to drink, but also to bathe and shower in, which can be reasonably easily done by acquiring a filter for the shower head, or even obtaining a whole house filter – more on this later. Filtered bathroom *Water* also substantially reduces mildew and moulds.

Even worse is fluoridated *Water*. 'But I thought it was good for our teeth' I hear you say. Well, research carried out in the 1930s told us that fluoride in drinking *Water* reduced the number of cavities in teeth by making the tooth enamel stronger. Fluoride however is a waste product of the aluminium industry and, like chlorine, is a poison which we do not want to be drinking in *Water* unless there is no suitable alternative!

Right! Enough of this doom and gloom and scare mongering. We could have a really good moan about all the pollutants in *Water* from industry and how our *Water* is being destroyed, but how stressful is that? Let's look at some potential solutions instead.

We clearly need to do our absolute best to campaign for industry to stop corrupting the *Water*s of our world if we get the opportunity.

We can improve tap *Water* by leaving it out overnight to allow some of the chlorine to evaporate away. We can boil it, then let it go cool, however the heating process does alter the structure of the *Water*, rendering it unnatural.

Putting a clear quartz crystal in the *Water* jug will help to energise and restructure the *Water*, as will standing the jug on a magnetic mat. For those of you who practice Reiki or anything similar, you can of course use your gift or skill to affect the *Water* beneficially, never mind our own thoughts, attitudes, intentions and emotions (more on this later).

Also, standing our *Water* in the sunshine will allow it to be energised by the far infra-red energy from the sun. Stirring our *Water* with a wooden spoon will energise it by creating a vortex.

## RAINWATER

Have you ever noticed that your dog (if you have one!) prefers to drink from puddles after a downpour, rather than your tap *Water* at home? Of course, it has no chlorine in it.

Rain can be saved after falling onto the roof by flowing through pipes to a storage tank. Any debris can be filtered out and small particles can be allowed to sink to the bottom. Any remaining floating debris can escape via an overflow pipe, and clean *Water* extracted from just below the surface. It can be used for *Water*ing the garden (good for plants because of the lack of chlorine), for flushing the toilet, for bathing and showering, and can be sterilised by an ultra violet unit before drinking.

## DISTILLED WATER

Distilled *Water* is made by boiling the *Water* and then condensing the steam. This gets rid of most impurities including fluoride, so it is easy to understand why it became a bit of a health fad back in the 1970s. It is so pure that it doesn't even have the dissolved minerals in it, so it has a very special ability to absorb toxic substances from our bodies and eliminate them. Because of this, Distilled *Water* may be very good to use *temporarily* as part of a de-toxification plan, but it is not recommended to be consumed regularly and especially not as our sole source of *Water*. In fact, it is said that drinking it all the time is highly detrimental. It is precisely because of its emptiness that it also has the potential to leach nutrients from our bodies too. When Distilled *Water* comes into contact with air, it absorbs carbon dioxide, which makes it acidic. As we see later, when thinking about filters, we do not want to be drinking acidic *Water*.

## BOTTLED WATERS

This is a more contentious area that attracts a range of opinions, so let's see how we can understand it better.

In short, spring *Water* comes from underground springs deep in the earth. Mineral *Water* is spring *Water* with a high mineral content due to the minerals in the land that it has passed over or through.

Sometimes the spring or mineral *Water*s are naturally carbonated, but even so, still *Water* is preferable due to the carbon dioxide in fizzy *Water*s, as consuming large amounts can unbalance the gases in our blood. We certainly do not want to be drinking *Water* that has been purposefully carbonated, other than on rare occasions.

Some (usually cheaper) bottled *Water*s are simply municipal *Water* that has been filtered and/or treated with ozone.

If we are going to need to drink bottled *Water* for a lengthy period of time for whatever reason, may I suggest that we choose a variety of different bottled *Water*s, as all will have differing proportions of minerals.

We can buy bottled *Water* in plastic or glass bottles, still or sparkling, plain or flavoured. May I suggest that we get rid of sparkling and flavoured *Water* straight away – the sparkling because of the carbon dioxide and the flavoured because as soon as we put anything into the *Water*, our bodies will treat it differently, needing to digest whatever is in the *Water* rather than just soaking it up and using it immediately.

So, the debate between plastic and glass. We are probably all going to buy *Water* in a plastic bottle from time to time, but let's try not to use *Water* from plastic bottles as our main source. We really, truly need to find a way to stop using so much plastics. Firstly, because there's the risk of some of the chemicals leaching from the plastics into the *Water*, especially if the plastic is quite flimsy and has been kept in warm conditions. There are chemicals that can leach out of plastic and interfere with our hormones as substances similar to oestrogens (hormones) leach from plastic under certain conditions. It doesn't really make sense to drink *Water* from a plastic bottle that is polluting the *Water*, if the reason for drinking it in the first place was to get away from the toxins in tap *Water*.

The sturdier the plastic, the better. To look at it the other way, the flimsier the plastic the more leaching of chemicals can happen.

Also, we can't get away from the environmental issue with plastics. There's the problem of all the oil and energy that is needed to make the plastic bottles in the first place, then the massive problem of getting rid of them! It seriously is a predicament and we radically need to reduce our use of plastic bottles. We are now finding plastic deposited over millions of square miles of the ocean floor ...how dreadful is that to the inhabitants of the seas and then consequently, to us?

*Glass* bottles are so much better! However, I appreciate that they are not always practical or financially viable for many of us to use as our sole source of *Water*. Glass bottles cost around double the amount of plastic and are both heavy and breakable. The *Water* however, is considerably better to drink.

Also, as we mentioned previously, in nature, *Water* flows – it doesn't stand still. I wonder how long some of the *Water* has been standing still whilst contained in the bottles, whether plastic or glass. Would you want to drink some tap or filtered *Water* that you had poured out days, if not weeks or months before?

I think I'd be correct in saying that many people who use bottled *Water* only tend to use it for drinking, and still continue putting tap *Water* in their kettle and using tap *Water* for cooking and washing their salad veggies. Ideally, we want to get away from tap *Water* altogether and I heartily encourage us all to consider other options rather than bottled *Water*s if it is possible for us to do so.

### FILTER BOTTLES

There are bottles which have a replaceable filter within them. These are a wonderful idea. They are portable and mean that we can refill them from the tap wherever we are, providing the tap *Water* is safe to drink. I have never needed to buy any bottled *Water* since getting mine.

### SPRING WATER STRAIGHT FROM SOURCE

Have a look at *www.findaspring.com* to find out if you are fortunate enough to have a natural spring nearby. You can search for springs anywhere in the world on this website and it is open to constantly hearing about new springs to put on their site, so please get in touch if you know of any near you! How wonderful to be able to go and fill up your containers (hopefully not plastic!) from *Water* that has been naturally filtered and energised by Mother Earth and bubbles out from an underground spring. Free of charge too!

## FILTERED WATER

Next... what about filters? I would love to be able to straightforwardly tell you which is the 'best' filter to have, but unfortunately it isn't as simple as that. With all sorts of shapes and sizes, price ranges and types available, I am simply going to give you a few basic guidelines so that you can research this area for yourself. Depending on your finances, you may want a jug type, the type that is attached to your tap or even a whole house system. It will also depend on what is available in your part of the world.

Most filters use carbon ash to filter out the impurities in *Water* – commonly known as charcoal. Charcoal is pretty much unsurpassed in its ability to absorb various pollutants, but in so doing it can also strip the *Water* of its natural minerals leaving the resulting *Water* with a pH level lower than neutral, i.e. acidic. Some filters will address this and naturally re-mineralise the *Water* before it emerges into the jug or out of the tap, but some of the simpler filters leave the *Water* acidic. All simple charcoal filters need to be replaced regularly because they can become a fantastic breeding ground for bacteria.

Reverse Osmosis units are extremely good at removing pollutants. I'd say they are probably the best at filtering out impurities but it is worth checking the resulting pH of the end *Water* before you

invest because of the possible removal of minerals too. The removal of minerals can leave the *Water* acidic. Reverse Osmosis does not need electricity but it does waste *Water*, using approximately 24 litres of *Water* for every four litres of *Water* that is 'cleaned'.

We can also find ionisers that separate *Water* into alkaline *Water* for drinking and acidic *Water* for using to wash hair and skin.

Clearly, the world of filters is a complex one. The motivation behind some *Water* filter manufacturers will be purely commercial, in that they simply want to make money whilst others have the health of their customers at heart.

In summary, I'd say one of the main issues to be clear on before investing in your filter, is the pH of the *Water* after filtering. As I mentioned above, some filters are very good at removing the 'rubbish' from the *Water*, but in doing this, they also strip the *Water* of its natural minerals, which can leave the *Water* acidic ...and we do not want to be drinking acidic *Water*! It may also be wise to question extremely alkaline *Water* if using it as one's sole source of *Water*, as with Distilled *Water*, it may be good to use as part of a treatment programme, but not really natural to drink it all the time. Mother Nature always knows best and if we were living a truly natural life then our *Water* would vary in its pH depending on the land it filtered through.

Also, in my opinion, the other main issue about the filter is whether it produces living, energised *Water*, as close to natural *Water* as we can possibly get. Some companies offer products to energise *Water* by creating a vortex. We can create a similar effect by stirring the *Water* vigorously with a wooden spoon.

We need to have a little chat about 'structured *Water*' too. Without getting too technical, it is all about the arrangement of the $H_2O$ molecules and the angle of the bond between the hydrogen and oxygen atoms ...well I thought you may be asking! Let me simply say that the more structured *Water* we have in our bodies, then the healthier we are going to be. The more structured the *Water*, the more energy it holds. Fruits and vegetables contain large amounts of structured *Water* too! If I tell you that *Water* can be structured by sunlight and by magnets, I wonder what you would immediately think? Well, it makes me quite emotional to once again realise that nature knows best and we will never ever improve on the amazing intelligence of Mother Nature! Remember what happens in the cycle of *Water*? It passes over the land as clouds, then it rains and has the sunlight beaming down on it, then it falls on the earth, which is a huge

magnet which energises the *Water*, creating 'Living *Water*.' Humbling.

As I said earlier, if you are in a position to be able to invest in a filter, then you are more likely to use that filtered *Water* for everything – drinking, putting in your kettle, cooking, washing your salad veggies, even possibly cleaning your teeth and as the drinking *Water* for your pets. If you buy bottled *Water*, would you agree the likelihood is that you will continue to use tap *Water* for everything other than drinking it? I would also recommend fitting a filter on your shower head in your bathroom. This is even better if you can also fill your bath through the shower head too, as I do.

In my opinion, the quality of the *Water* we drink has the greatest effect on our health than any other substance we will ever put in our bodies. Surely, therefore, it makes sense to source the highest quality *Water* that is possible for us to drink; to make it one of our top priorities and then to drink enough of it!

*'Anyone who thinks that sunshine is pure happiness, has never danced in the rain.'*

48

# 11

## MOVING INSIDE

Now we have some information about the types of *Water* available to us to help us choose which *Water* to drink. Is there anything else we can do to help towards hydrating ourselves?

The answer is... 'Yes, lots!'

Even if you are not familiar with the power of visualisation and the power of your thoughts, still have a go at this.

Take a glass of clean, pure, still *Water*, or as clean and pure as you can get.

*Listen* to the *Water* as it flows into your glass from your tap, jug or bottle. Notice its gentle sound, imagine it flowing through beautiful countryside.

*Hold* your glass between your hands and be aware of the energy you have in those hands that can be transmitted to the *Water* in your glass.

*Appreciate* the *Water*, feeling gratitude for having clean *Water* when so many human beings are not as fortunate. Imagine imprinting the *Water* with your gratitude.

*Look* at it. Notice its clarity, its fluidity, its movement, its energy – how it takes the shape of whatever vessel you have poured it into. Hold it up to the light and see the light shine right through it.

Hold it up to your nose and *smell* it. Does it have a smell? Hopefully not chlorine! Does it have a freshness to it?

Take a mouthful and *feel* its texture. Really notice the sensations as though this is the first time you have ever experienced this most amazing of all substances, the source of life itself. Roll it around your mouth, enjoying the temperature changes, the wetness, the refreshing feelings against every inch of soft tissue lining your mouth and throat.

I wonder if you can *taste* it. Certainly as you become more used to drinking good quality, more natural *Water*, you will become a bit of a connoisseur of *Water* and you will be able to detect chlorine a mile away! You will gradually begin to enjoy the subtleties in the differing flavours of *Water*, aware of the various tastes from the different varieties of bottled *Water*s and the range of filtered *Water*s right through to natural Spring *Water*s.

Allow yourself to begin to have an awareness of the exceptional qualities of this liquid that you are about to swallow, consciously reminding yourself that every cell in your entire body wants and needs a regular supply of this colourless nectar ultimately remembering that you are basically made of it.

Let yourself now swallow your mouthful of *Water*. As you feel it flowing down through your throat and oesophagus on its way into your stomach, use the power of your imagination to visualise this *Water* sending a reassuring message of hydration through your body. Some of the *Water* will be absorbed directly into your body from your stomach and some will move through your stomach into your small intestine. It really doesn't matter how you imagine it – your insides don't need to look like they have just come out of an anatomy book! Picture the inside of you however you want to, as long as it's personal to you. Think about the *Water* sending a lovely, soothing, reassuring message to every part of your body, maybe like a relay message saying, 'It's OK! Lots of *Water* is coming regularly so you can relax now and be happy!'

The whole of our gastro-intestinal tract is lined with mucous membranes. Remember that we all have receptors in the lining of our colon (also called Large Intestine or Bowel) which pick up the message as to whether there's a drought going on in the body or not. We want to reassure these receptors more than anything that there is a constant supply of *Water* coming in. Picture your receptors, again in any way that you want to, being soothed and calmed and having their mind put at rest.

To some of you, this may sound a little crazy and ridiculous, but maybe not to others who are very aware of the power of our minds in influencing our bodies. Recent research helps us to understand the whole mind/body connection so much more clearly now, which is a completely fascinating subject all of its own. I'd really encourage you to have a look at some of the 'New Biology' in terms of 'Epigenetics' and also the 'Law of Attraction' philosophy if you are interested.

My simple suggestion is to not only drink the *Water*, but also visualise it doing the job we want it to do, knowing that every thought we have is instantaneously communicated to every cell in our body at the speed of light.

# 12

## THE HUG IN A MUG

Another way to help towards hydrating ourselves is an age old recipe for a beverage called linseed or flaxseed tea. At college, we refer to this drink as 'A Hug In A Mug' and it really is pure hydration. It is absolutely ideal for reassuring those receptors! For those of you who are Flaxseed Tea Virgins, may I strongly encourage you to persevere with it. Slowly but surely is the way forward, without having to drink copious amounts to begin with. My very first experience of Linseed/Flaxseed Tea was not the best, as I really hated it. However, very, very quickly, I grew to love it and I'm sure you will eventually agree with me that it is the most comforting, soothing, hot drink you could ever wish for. So get to love it just like I do, because your body will love it.

Whilst Flaxseeds and Linseeds are grown in different parts of the world, they are very similar. There are both the golden and dark brown varieties of seed, and as far as I am aware, they are equally beneficial. The main rule of thumb is to use whichever is more indigenous to you.

When the seeds are put in *Water*, the oil is drawn out of the seeds and makes a gloopy texture. We call this 'thickened *Water*' and it's this wonderful mucilaginous texture that contributes to the soothing reassurance referred to earlier. This 'thickened *Water*' message helps to tell the receptors in our gut that there is no drought going on, so our body can switch off the mechanism we call dehydration alert. Hence the 'Hug In a Mug' is born..

There are two ways you can make this... the best way and a close second best way.

## BEST WAY

1. In a large pan, (please do not use aluminium) put two tablespoons of whole, organic linseeds or flaxseeds (golden or brown or a mixture) and pour in one litre of good quality *Water*.

2. Bring it to the boil.

3. Put a lid on the pan and switch off the heat.

4. Leave to stand overnight for about 12 hours.

You can happily drink up to 500mls per day, on top of your two litres of *Water*.

You may prefer to make it more diluted from the start, in which case, use more *Water* or less seeds in the pan. You will soon get used to your preferred way of making it.

### A CLOSE SECOND BEST WAY

1. Invest in a good quality thermos flask.

2. Before going to bed, put two tablespoons of whole seeds into a family sized flask.

3. Fill with boiling *Water* and screw the top on tightly.

4. Leave overnight.

5. Take your flask with you wherever you may be going during the day and drink it ...seeds and all if you wish, but remember, *no seeds if you have Diverticulitis*.

6. If you don't consume the seeds, you may use them for a second time.

5. Take the lid off, bring to the boil again and gently simmer for an hour. Do not let it boil over or else you will get a real sticky mess on the top of the stove that is the devil to get off!

6. Pour through a sieve to discard the seeds. (Eat them if you really want to, by all means, by putting them in soup for example, but *do not eat the seeds if you have Diverticulitis*.)

Your resulting linseed/flaxseed tea will be very thick at this point. Add hot *Water* to make it the consistency you want to drink it. Once cooled, keep it in the fridge then add hot *Water* when you are going to drink it. If there's still any left after three days, throw it away, but hopefully there won't be any left!

# 13

## GOOD VIBRATIONS

My final thoughts for you are possibly the most exciting ones of all. Possibly for some of you, also the least easy ones to believe and take on board. I encourage you simply to be as open minded as possible as you continue to read, bearing in mind that you can dismiss it if you want to; even skip over it if it sounds too far-fetched! Having said that, you can authenticate it by doing some further research yourself, and even better, experiment yourself and prove it one way or another. I can't say fairer than that.

To begin to understand how we can influence the quality of our *Water* ourselves, first we need to have a little talk about vibration. Let's keep it really simple because there's no need to complicate it. Up to the 1940s or so, the world of science (which includes all of us,

I suppose) believed that everything was solid (apart from liquids and gases of course!) This was based on the work of Newton. We've come a long way from then, and science has moved forward in leaps and bounds in our knowledge and understanding of what everything, including ourselves, is made from. Basically, everything is made from molecules, which in turn are made from things that you will no doubt have heard of, such as atoms and these atoms have subatomic particles. Given our technology at this point in time, there's only so far we can go to see things as small as we can, so when the scientists get their electron microscopes out and use their dark field microscopy, they can peer deep inside our cells. When they go as deep as they possibly can do, what do they find? The answer is: lots of space and vibrating particles called protons, neutrons and electrons amongst others. Sounds crazy I know! In fact everything is made of particles vibrating at different frequencies. Different colours have different frequencies. Different foods have different frequencies. For example, a cucumber will vibrate at around 200megahertz, whereas some denatured, processed foods will be around as little as three or four perhaps. Emotions too have frequencies. We are told that the highest vibrational emotions are those of love, appreciation and gratitude. OK? That's enough about vibrations! I can just imagine some of you thinking, 'Come on, hurry up and get to the point!' OK, I will.

A Japanese gentleman called Masaru Emoto has carried out loads of experiments by exposing different samples of *Water* to different vibrations. He spoke lovingly to some of the *Water* samples whilst conversely hurling abuse at others. He played various music, exposed the *Water* to different coloured glass containers and even wrote words on paper and either stood the *Water* on them or stuck the written words onto the vessels holding the *Water*. He then froze the *Water* and analysed the resulting ice crystals. I can tell you that the results are astonishing! You may like to go and find them for yourself. It's really fascinating stuff! In a nutshell, the ice crystals from the *Water* exposed to higher vibrations such as love were perfectly formed, beautiful and exquisite. The ones exposed to lower vibrations such as hate were misshapen, malformed and ugly.

Something you can try for yourself is to buy two identical plants (or as identical as you can get) and keep them in a similar place. *Water* them with different *Water*. Have two jugs of *Water* which you keep fairly separate – perhaps in different rooms. Speak lovingly to one of the jugs of *Water* several times a day and tell it how gorgeous it is and how much you love it (No, I'm not on drugs!) Do the opposite to the other jug of *Water* by telling it how much you hate and despise it – not very nice really, but all in a good cause. Perhaps even more effective is to simply ignore that *Water* and say nothing to it. Keep it going for at least a couple of weeks, maybe even as long as a month and observe the differences with the plants. You can do it again and again to satisfy yourself and if you genuinely carry it out as I have suggested, then you will also get astonishing results.

You can also carry out a similar experiment by *Water*ing one plant with cooled microwaved *Water* and one with *Water* which has not been microwaved. The results will encourage you to throw away your microwave and certainly never ever heat your *Water* in it.

This surely means that *Water* is affected in a positive or negative way by every vibration it encounters. This must also mean that this is happening when it is both outside of us and *inside* of us!

So, given that we are all made largely of *Water* and *Water* is clearly affected by the vibrations it encounters, then it begs the question, 'How powerful are our thoughts and the language we use when we speak to ourselves in affecting the *Water* once it is inside us?' It would seem apparent that being critical and hard on ourselves is going to affect the *Water* in our bodies in a negative way, just as being caring and loving towards ourselves will be affecting us in a healthy and positive way. Woweee!

By knowing that we all have the ability to affect the *Water* we drink by our thoughts, words and our intentions, surely this helps to take away some of the helplessness that we are constantly being encouraged to feel from the media when we are bombarded with information regarding how polluted our *Water* is.

Bearing this in mind, no matter what our financial situation, we can all go some way to improving the quality of the *Water* we are drinking.

In view of all of this, our focus needs not only to be on the quality of *Water* we drink, but also on how we influence that *Water* as it passes through us and finally leaves us to continue flowing on its journey through Earth and her inhabitants.

It's not always easy to think positively, but it does become so much easier to think more clearly as we become more hydrated. As our internal stress reduces, then we experience less 'Fight, Flight or Freeze' symptoms and consequently the blood supply to our frontal cortex in our brain increases, hence we have a greater ability to think properly rather than just reacting. As we start thinking more clearly, then we can actively learn to choose more useful, better feeling thoughts. This becomes easier and easier as it gradually becomes more habitual to look for the positive in every situation (easier said than done, I know!) Imagine how our health and happiness can increase in leaps and bounds when we get to this point. When our thoughts, which are affecting every drop of *Water*

inside of us, are more loving and appreciative, when we are actively transmitting higher vibrational thoughts to every cell in our bodies throughout every second of every day, how powerful can we be?

How far and wide can this message spread? What if the farmers of the world and the growers of our food took this on board and created the healthiest *Water* possible to *Water* our fruits and vegetables, the grass that the animals eat and the *Water* that they drink? What about the health of the rivers and streams, seas and oceans that flow through our land? In theory, taken to the nth degree, this really can start to raise the vibration of our entire planet. It is up to us – you and me – to take the time and make the effort to do it and spread the word for others to do it too. There doesn't seem to be a drawback to this at all. I can't think of any negatives whatsoever, only amazing benefits for the whole of Mother Earth and all the living creatures who depend on her.

What a wonderful, humbling cycle it is of *Water* and life, constantly circulating, flowing and changing. Sometimes stagnant, polluted, filthy and dead. Sometimes clean, pure, energised, magnificent, wise and alive, affected by and affecting everything it comes into contact with.

We are all in this together.

Between us, we *can* all contribute towards improving the health of *Water* alongside improving our own health and happiness.

# 14

## ROUNDING UP

I hope it has become crystal clear to you how crucially important *Water* is in your own health and happiness. Without question, *Water* holds the key to the health and happiness of all living creatures.

It also seems to be true that we humans hold the key to the health and happiness of *Water*. If we are an image of the world outside us; if we are the microcosms within the macrocosm, then could it be that we live in symbiotic union with *Water*?

In nearing the end of my book, let's have a little recap on the topics we have covered:

As we have sailed through the chapters, we have discovered a little more about *Water*, why it is so very important for all living beings, how we lose it and gain it. We have looked at the issue of stress and how this is the most dehydrating thing of all. I hope you now have an understanding of the need to bridge the gap between the amount we lose every day and the amount we gain. I'm sure you were overawed by how magnificently our bodies try to deal with dehydration. We discussed our 'Natural Thirst Mechanism' and how simple but wonderful it is to kick-start it and to be able to assist the children of our world to kick-start theirs too. Having a sensible guideline to get you started, along with an idea of the possible consequences of hydrating, perhaps you are now inspired to get going! We went through a general guide to the kinds of *Water* which are available to many people, so I hope this will be helpful in making your choices. Remember to get to love the 'Hug In A Mug' too. We ventured into how *Water* is affected by every vibration it encounters and, I have every faith in you all now, that you will begin to use the incredible power of your own thoughts to influence *Water* as it passes through you.

I'd like to emphasise our role in affecting *Water* as it passes through us. It's an area and subject that is rarely talked about.

The more clogged up we are inside, the more stagnant the *Water* becomes. The 'cleaner' we are, the more space we have inside, then the more freedom of movement we have for the *Water* to flow through our lymph, veins, arteries and capillaries to our cells and the more energised that *Water* will become. Think about liquefied food passing through our 20-odd feet of tubing that is our small intestine. In health this becomes like a vortex and creates energy too. Likewise, blood flows through our heart in a figure of eight. Just writing this sends a shiver up my spine. NATURE IS AMAZING!

Our health and happiness depends on the health and happiness of our *Water* and vice versa, because all living creatures share this wonderful, amazing, mysterious, life giving liquid crystal we call *Water*.

In closing this book, I truly hope that you have enjoyed reading it and have felt totally involved just as though we've been sitting together over a lovely hydrating mug of Flaxseed Tea having a good natter.

I invite you to read it over and over again until you reach that 'Aha' moment when the penny drops, the light bulb switches on and you suddenly 'Get it!' When the realisation of the role of *Water* really dawns on you. When the realisation of the power you have also dawns on you...

*...That you can actually gradually move towards being more hydrated,* *which is the start of the solution to everything.*

Once you understand the things we have chatted about, then if you wish to, you can immediately make a start on your own personal hydration journey. You do not need to go to someone else to do this for you. Without being obsessed you can make it a focus of every day to drink *Water*, reducing other substances that are dehydrating, challenging and stressful to your body. Gradually, you may emerge from the prune into the plum. Gradually, you may feel less and less anxious. Gradually, you may be able to think more clearly. Gradually, you may feel more energised. Gradually you may be able to choose more positive thoughts. This is all because you are steadily becoming more and more hydrated – reassuring your cells (which are you) that there is no drought going on, that they are getting a constant, regular supply of *Water* and that you are not living in the desert.

Please don't think that I'm saying that hydration is the answer to everything, but I am suggesting that it is the start of the answer to everything. It is the foundation that greater health and happiness can be built on and without switching off 'dehydration alert' then very little improvement in health will happen.

I encourage you with every cell in my being to act on the information in this book. I also ask you to share and spread this information far and wide with belief and conviction borne from your own experience, with enthusiasm, with inspiration and a passion to empower others to also become healthier and happier with *Water*.

Let's raise our glasses of exquisite *Water* in a toast to all other human beings and living creatures who inhabit the Earth.

'In gratitude and appreciation we thank you *Water*. You connect us all. You truly are *The Elixir of Life*.'

*Cheers!*

## ABOUT THE AUTHOR

Lesley Una Pierce lives in Lancashire, England where she is a partner of **The Nutritional Healing Foundation** *www.nutrihealfoundation.com* She teaches students how to improve their health and happiness naturally by practising the Naturopathic Philosophy she is so passionate about, having fully incorporated it into her own life.

Lesley became attracted to alternative methods of prevention and cure after working as a student nurse at **St. James's University Hospital** in Leeds. She qualified as a *Hypno-Psychotherapist* and *NLP Master Practitioner* in the early nineties and worked in the complementary therapy clinics of local hospices and in her own private practice before becoming involved with **The Nutritional Healing Foundation** in 2004.

## ACKNOWLEDGEMENTS

Thank you, thank you, *thank you* to my wonderful family, partners and friends. You know who you are. I appreciate you all.

Special thanks to: my son, James Pierce, for his skill in proof reading and doing the initial editing, to Tony Clarkson at *The Sanctuary of Healing* for his help in slotting everything into place beautifully and to my publishers *Sanctuary Press* for their much needed, fabulous, professional advice.

I feel very blessed to have an abundance of gorgeous people in my life. In gratitude to everyone who has inspired me along the way.

Thank you.